THE LAST SELCHIE CHILD

JANE YOLEN

D0543245

FABULA RASA 04

A MIDSUMMER NIGHT'S PRESS

New York

Main cover photo ©2011 M. A. Mathews (alberich@valkyries.com)

A Midsummer Night's Press
16 West 36th Street
2ns Floor
New York, NY 10018
amidsummernightspress@gmail.com
www.amidsummernightspress.com

Grateful acknowledgement is given to the editors of the following publications in which many of these poems first appeared (sometimes in a different form): *The Armless Maiden* (edited by Terri Windling, Tor Books): "The Mirror Speaks"; *Asimov's Science Fiction Magazine:* "Fairies in a Ring", "Foxwife", "Garden Fairies", "Green Children", "Into the Wood", "Tower"; *Coyote Road: Trickster Tales* (edited by Ellen Datlow & Terri Windling, Viking): "Kwaku Anansi"; *Doorways Magazine:* "Beauty Sleep" and "Petit Rouge Grows Old"; The Faery Flag (by Jane Yolen, Philomel): "Beauty and the Beast: An Anniversary"; *Golbin Fruit:* "The Selchie Children's Plaint"; *Jabberwocky:* "Black Dog Times"; *Marvels and Tales: A Journal:* "Märchen"; *National Storyteller's Journal:* "Family Stories", "Once Upon a Time (She Said)", "Story", "The Storyteller"; *Once Upon A Time (She Said)* (by Jane Yolen, NESFA Press): "Beans"; *Orphans of the Night* (edited by Josepha Sherman, Walker Books): "Great Selkie"; *Peregrine:* "When Raven Sang"; *Sisters in Fantasy* (edited by Susan Schwartz, Roc Books): "Women's Stories"; *Snow White, Blood Red* (edited by Ellen Datlow & Terri Windling, Avon): "Knives"; *Star*Line:* "The Fates" and "Ridinghood"; *Tales of Wonder* (by Jane Yolen, Schocken Books): "Prince Charming Comes"; *A World of Literature:* "Glass Slipper"; *Xanadu* (edited by Jane Yolen, Tor Books): "The Ring at Yarrow"; *Xanadu 2* (edited by Jane Yolen, Tor Books): "Orkney Lament"; *Xanadu 3* (edited by Jane Yolen, Tor Books): "Swan/Princess". "Long Sleep" is original to this collection.

"Will" and "This is a Story" were first published as a limited edition hand-printed broadside from A Midsummer Night's Press in 1992.

Designed by Aresográfico www.diegoareso.com

First edition, Mayo 2012.

ISBN-13: 978-0-9794208-9-4
ISBN-10: 0-9794208-9-X

Printed in Spain.

CONTENTS

1.
Story

"Because each of us tells
the same story
but tells it differently"
> —Lisel Mueller, "Why We Tell Stories"

THE STORYTELLER

He unpacks his bag of tales
with fingers quick
as a weaver's
     picking the weft threads,
     threading the warp.
Watch his fingers.
Watch his lips
speaking the old familiar words:

> *"Once there was*
> *and there was not,*
> *oh, best beloved,*
> *when the world was filled with wishes*
> *the way the sea is filled with fishes…"*

All those threads
pulling us back
to another world, another time,
when goosegirls married well
and frogs could rhyme,
when maids spoke syllables of pearl
and stepmothers came to grief.

Belief is the warp

and the sharp-picked pattern
of motif
reminds us that Araby
is not so far;
that the pleasure dome
of a Bagdad caliph
sits side by side
with the rush-roofed home
of a Tattercoat or an animal bride.
Cinderella wears a shoe
first fitted in the East
where her prince--
no more a beast
than the usual run of royal son--
measures her nobility
by the lotus foot,
so many inches to the reign.
Then the slipper made glass
by a slip of ear and tongue.
All tales are mistakes
made true by the telling.

The watching eye takes in the hue,
the listening ear the word,
but all they comprehend is Art.
A story must be worn again
before the magic garment

fits the ready heart.

The storyteller is done.
He packs his bag.
But watch his fingers
and his lips.
It is the oldest feat
of prestidigitation.
What you saw,
what you heard
was equal to a new Creation.

The colors blur,
time is now.
He speaks his final piece
before his final bow:

> *"It is all true,*
> *it is not true.*
> *The more I tell you,*
> *the more I shall lie.*
> *What is story*
> *but jesting Pilate's cry.*
> *I am not paid to tell you the truth."*

MÄRCHEN

Wilhelm Grimm loved words,
not stories,
they waterfalled from his pen.
He was deaf to the telling,
only the told.

Words like camphor.
goblet, ruby, anvil
waxed and waned in him.
He was tidal
with words.

I, on the other hand,
drink in tales,
giving them out again
in mouth-to-ear
resuscitation.

It does not matter
if the matter of the stories
is the coast of Eire
or the Inland Sea,
I swim--ah--ever deeper in them.

RIDINGHOOD

Writers wear their craft
like a ridinghood, proudly,
saying: See--I am an artist,
What do I care
for money. Except
to live on. And on. And on.
I publish that my soul
not perish.
Ask my agent,
that resident wolf.
Ten percent teeth,
five percent howl.
She goes to bed with editors,
rises up again
with a muzzle full of fleas.
One day I shall have to kill her.
It is an old story.

STORY

Somewhere between
My lips, your ear,
Is the story
You should hear.

But that is not
The tale you find.
You shape a tale
To fit your mind.

And so it goes,
In re-creation,
Mouth-to-ear
Resuscitation,

Resurrecting
Tales we hear.
Truth lies between
The mouth and ear.

ONCE UPON A TIME (SHE SAID)

"Once upon a time," she said,
and the world began anew:
a vee of geese flew by,
plums roasting in their breasts;
a vacant-eyed princess
sat upon a hillock of glass;
a hut strolled through a tangled wood,
the nails on its chickenfeet
blackened and hard as coal;
a horse's head proclaimed advice
from the impost of an arch;
one maiden spoke in toads,
another in pearls,
and a third with the nightingale's voice.
If you ask me,
I would have to say
all the world's magic
comes directly from the mouth.

2.
Stories

___

"Man the story-teller would have
to be redeemed in a manner consonant
with his nature: by a moving story."
                    —J.R.R. Tolkien in a letter to his son

THE LAST SELCHIE CHILD

Mother, after you left,
your skin wrapped tight around you,
my brothers, my sisters
waded into the water
till the tide caught them,
and they were gone.
You never taught us how to swim,
how to breathe underwater.
You never wanted us
to go near the sea.
Now I am left in the little cottage
with the mosses in the chinks
that keep it warm in the winter
and cool in the summer.
But I am the last selchie child,
my blood runs cold in my veins
like an onrushing tide.
If I go to the water's edge,
if I stick my feet in the foam,
will you be there to catch me,
to breathe into my mouth?
Or will you just let me drift
down, down, down to the sandy bottom,
with all the sea reflected in my eyes?

ORKNEY LAMENT

When Magnus swam easy in his blood
And the selkies sang his passing,
No one in the islands was surprised.
Living is the miracle, not death.
Between the ice and axe
Lies but little space.

> There were dolphins at the bow,
> And tunny down below.
> Earl Magnus is the sea.

When Magnus flew silent in his blood
And the curlews cried his passing,
No one on the islands was surprised.
Peace is the awkwardness, not war.
Between the hawk and hand
Lies but a shield of skin.

> There were eagles at the prow,
> And osprey at the oars.
> Earl Magnus is the dove.

When Magnus fell saintly in his blood
And the oxen wept at his passing,

No one on the islands was surprised.
Growing is the prodigy, not rot.
Between stalk and root
Lies but a shaft of green.

> There were blossoms on the bough
> And petals on the ground.
> Earl Magnus is the seed.

GREAT SELKIE

When he came courting, Jesus,
he was a lovely man,
his face smooth and sly,
his hair the color of plums.
I plucked yarrow to keep me safe.
> *"May I be an isle in the sea,*
> *May I be a hill on the shore."*

We danced on heather all in darkness,
his body against mine,
till we were wet as water,
till I breathed in salt.
> *"May I be a star in waning of the moon."*

The yarrow wilted before dawn.
All crested and furred,
he returned to the sea.
I was not honest with him;
he was not my first.
But I will a child of him,
webbings between its fingers
grey as storm air,
Then we shall see who is queen of the isle.
We shall see who claims the Selkie's trove.

THE SELCHIE'S CHILDREN'S PLAINT

In the box a gray skin,
wrinkled like the turning tide,
smelling of salt and old blood.
Unsmiling, Mama picks it up,
slings it over her shoulders
where it shapes itself to her back.
She leaves us then, without a word
wading into her future.
It hurts like a knife
skinning us as we watch her go.
We were the ones
who were to dive into another life.
But Mama goes first, leaving us
with only a box empty of promises
and a cold kitchen.

BALLAD OF THE WHITE SEAL MAID

The fisherman sits alone on the land,
His hands are his craft, his boat is his art,
The fisherman sits alone on the land,
A rock, a rock in his heart.

The selchie maid swims alone in the bay,
Her eyes are the seal's, her heart is the sea,
The selchie maid swims alone through the bay,
A white seal maid is she.

She comes to the shore and sheds her seal skin,
She dances on the sand and under the moon,
Her hair falls in waves all down her white skin,
Only the seals her the tune.

The fisherman stands and takes up her skin,
Staking his claim to a wife from the sea,
He raises his hand and holds up the skin,
"Now you must come home with me."

Weeping she goes and weeping she stays,
Her hands are her craft, her babes are her art,
A year and a year and a year more she stays,
A rock, a rock in her heart.

But what is this hid in the fisherman's bag?
It smells of the ocean, it feels like the sea,
A bony-white seal skin closed up in the bag,
And never a tear more sheds she.

"Good-bye to the house and good-bye to the shore,
Good-bye to the babes that I never could claim.
But never a thought to the man left on shore,
For selchie's my nature and name."

She puts on the skin and dives back in the sea,
The fisherman's cry falls on water-deaf ears.
She swims in her seal skin far out to the sea.
The fisherman drowns in his tears.

FOXWIFE

I found him, my gentle scholar,
living in a ruined temple.
If he can stand my cooking—
the meat too rare for most—
and my rank smell,
if he can forgive the sight
of my red tail,
I will make him a good wife.
Beast or girl,
I pledge him a warm fire
and quiet for his studies
long into the night,
and any who disturb him
will know my teeth.

KWAKU ANANSI WALKS
THE WORLD'S WEB

Come a-walking
Kwaku Anansi, the spider man,
Come a-walking
Kwaku Anansi, the tricksy one.
He brings stories from the sky god,
So we may learn beginnings,
so we may learn endings.
He brings us the sun, the moon, the rains,
The division between day and night.
He brings the small grains
And the shovel.
He tricks us into believing in ourselves,
In our brains, our hearts, our pulses.
He teaches us to unlock locked boxes,
To grab the calabash of life,
To be clever if we cannot be wise,
To star in our own (hi)stories.
He teaches us how to fling ourselves
Into the void, using only the web.
Come-a-walking,
Kwaku Anansi, and tell us a tale.

GLASS SLIPPER

How silly. Glass
 would cut my feet to ribbons,
  little scarlet ribbons,
   marking my path
    all the way home.
     And even if they did not break
      they would never get comfortable,
       molding themselves
        to the bumps and bevels of my toes.
         No prince is worth the pain.
          Besides—I want to dance
           all night.

BEAUTY SLEEP

Oh, I've had trouble sleeping
since you died, dreams
of you dead in the bed
keep me awake. One kiss,
one last kiss, might let me go.
But you were my only prince
and now you're gone.
Gone where? God knows.
And she isn't telling.
I tell you, that's some gig,
always stealing someone else's prince.

LONG SLEEP

I slept through the alarm,
Past the first day of school,
Past birthdays,
                    movie dates,
                                    puberty.
I went from childhood to old age,
Rompers to size twelve
With no intermediate steps,
Waiting for a prince.

Don't tell me it was worth it.

KNIVES

Love can be as sharp
as the point of a knife,
as piercing as a sliver of glass.
My sisters did not know this.
They thought love was an old slipper:
pull it on and it fits.
They did not know this secret of the world:
the wrong word can kill.
It cost them their lives.

Princes understand the world,
they know the nuance of the tongue,
they are bred up in it.
A shoe is not a shoe:
it implies miles, it suggests length,
it measures and makes solid,
it wears and is worn.
Where there is one shoe, there must be a match.
Otherwise the kingdom limps along.

Glass is not glass
in the language of love:
it implies sight, it suggests depth,
it mirrors and makes real,

it is sought and seen.
What is made of glass reflects the gazer.
A queen must be made of glass.

I spoke to the prince in that secret tongue,
the diplomacy of courting.
he using shoes, I using glass,
and all my sisters saw was a slipper,
too long in the heel,
too short at the toe.
What else could they use but a knife?
What else could he see but the declaration of war?

Princes understand the world,
they know the nuance of the tongue,
they are bred up to it.
In war as in life they take no prisoners
and they always marry the other shoe.

THE MIRROR SPEAKS

I have reflected upon abuse
all of my life,
and the vanity of loving.
Mothers see their worth
in the bones of a child,
in soft ligaments, gentle curves
like new-formed planets
not yet jutting into rock.
"Was I ever so fair?" they ask.
"Was I ever so new?"

> *I cannot speak lies,*
> *but each truth is half-told;*
> *hot is not warm, but warming,*
> *age by planet's count not old.*

Where does the threat begin—
in the cradle? In the heart?
Under the breastbone?
Behind the eyes,
where the time-crow plants
its uncaring feet, toes splayed,
etching the fine lines?
I show you what you would see:

bleached eyes, yellow teeth,
the lines of grey hair.
You were never so fair.

> *I cannot speak lies,*
> *but each truth is half-told;*
> *hot is not warm but warming,*
> *green is but part of gold.*

Is it the child's fault?
Is it the glass?
Is it the fault of winter
and summer and winter again?
All childhoods pass.
I have reflected upon abuse
All of my life.
The answer is truth:
oh queen, all Snow Whites
are fairer still,
as you were, in your youth.

> *I cannot speak lies,*
> *but each truth is half-told;*
> *hot is not warm but warming,*
> *death is but cool, not cold.*

BEAUTY AND THE BEAST: AN ANNIVERSARY

It is winter now,
and the roses are blooming again,
their petals bright against the snow.
My father died last April;
my sisters no longer write
except at the turnings of the year,
content with their fine houses
and their grandchildren.
Beast and I putter in the gardens
and walk slowly on the forest paths.
He is graying
around the muzzle
and I have silver combs
to match my hair.
I have no regrets.
None.
Though sometimes I do wonder
what sounds children
might have made
running across the marble halls,
swinging from the birches
over the roses
in the snow.

TOWER

I stare at the stones,
grey as my days
and the little gray mouse
who has found its way in.
A lifetime I am to stay
with only you to hear my prayers
and carry them out
through the holes in the thick walls.
My fingernails are broken now;
I cannot attempt another escape.
But I have found
the small barred window,
where I sing each morning
to any passing prince.
Be he large or small, handsome or plain,
I will have him.
Pride and honor are broken now
on this rack of grey.

WILL

The past will not lie buried.
Little bones and teeth
harrowed from grave's soil,
tell different tales.
My father's bank box told me,
in a paper signed by his own hand,
the name quite clearly: William.
All the years he denied it,
that name, that place of birth,
that compound near Kiev,
and I so eager for the variants
with which he lived his life.
In the middle of my listening,
death,
that old interrupter,
with the unkindness of all coroners,
revealed his third name to me.
Not William, not Will, but Wolf.
Wolf.
And so at last I know the story,
my old wolf, white against the Russian snows,
the cracking of his bones,
the stretching sinews,
the coarse hair growing boldly

on the belly, below the eye.
Why grandfather, my children cry,
what great teeth you have,
before he devours them
as he devoured me,
all of me, bones and blood,
all of my life.

THE FATES

Fire shadows on the wall,
A hand rises, falls, as steady as a heart beat,
Threading the strands of life.
This is the warp thread, this the woof,
This the hero-line, this the fool.

>   *Needle and scissors, scissors and pins,*
>   *Where one life ends, another begins.*

There was a hero, once, from Ithica.
See how he travels the road.
Dust devils up under his bare feet.
The pattern in the dust is plainweave,
Is herringweave, is twill.

>   *Needle and scissors, scissors and pins,*
>   *Where one life ends, another begins.*

So quickly the shuttle flies,
As fast as an arrow to the heart,
As fast as the poison of the asp,
As fast as the sword blade against the neck,
As fast as life, as fast as death.

> *Needle and scissors, scissors and pins,*
> *Where one life ends, another begins.*

Did the silkworm come first,
Spinning its cocoon tapestry
So Clotho could unspin its cloak home
Into one of her own?
Did the Morai learn from a worm?

> *Needle and scissors, scissors and pins,*
> *Where one life ends, another begins.*

Or did she come upon flax as a girl
And, seduced by its bright blue flowers,
Blue as the branching veins beneath the fragile shield of skin,
Crush it into fiber and thread?

> *Needle and scissors, scissors and pins,*
> *Where one life ends, another begins.*
> *Needle and scissors, scissors and pins,*
> *Where one life ends, another begins.*
> *Spindle and rod and tablet and thread,*
> *The scissors close—and you are dead.*

GARDEN FAIRIES

There are fairies in my garden,
not the bottom but near the front end,
gnawing on the long stems of roses,
their teeth sharper than the thorns.
Do not let them know you see them
or they will disappear into a swollen petal
or beat their wings in time
to the hummingbird's tune
till you cannot tell one from the other.
Be careful you do not smell of flowers,
or honey, or possibly of fruit.
Leave off perfumes when you go there.
Shampoos must be chosen with care:
mint will do, or pine tar.
If they smell something sweet,
they will sink their teeth
into your flesh, and you will become
a mooncalf, a ninnywit, a scare-bird
howling at the stars.
My uncle was taken that way,
here in the garden, a year ago Friday.
I would not want it happening to you.

PETIT ROUGE GROWS OLD

A red spot on each cheek,
eyes lined in kohl,
nipples rouged,
perfume in all my hidden spaces,
I go out into the forest.
The wolves are howling,
a rise and fall of sound.
The sunset plunges.
I feel it in my throat.
I walk the path,
One foot on, one off,
Not afraid, but wary,
perhaps not wary but weary.
It has been two years since
my woodcutter husband died.
But like many a dried fruit
I am still sweet.

GETTING OLD THE MYTHIC WAY

GREEN MAN GROWN OLD

Wrists veined like leaves,
Hair the color of flowers gone by,
He bends with every passing wind.
He can no longer lie with a lover,
Nor dance inside the storm.
Too much hail hurts his hide.
The swollen river makes his right ankle seize up.
He is always thirsty, even in the rain.
Yet he does not complain.
He does not complain.

LAST UNICORN

Others, like foxes, go to ground,
But the last unicorn, whitened,
Faded the color of old sheets hung
On a trailer park line,
Goes to the edge of the ocean.
The tops of waves are as white as he.
Brothers, he thinks, sisters,

And plunges in, not so much a death
As a transfiguration.

AT LAST, THE LITTLE MERMAID

She no longer remembers the knives in her feet,
Or the one in her hand, so close to his throat
It might have pricked him without her meaning to.
She no longer remembers the curse
Or the cure or the painful interstices.
All she remembers is foam, the bubbles rising,
And the songs of angels,
So like the murmuration of the sea.

JACK, THE GIANT, AND ALL AFTER

Two old men, playing chess, in a house of old men.
As they play a harp keeps them company.
They share a history, though neither can recall it.
One so large, his memories are all of sky.
The other so small, he thinks all day of earth.
Two old friends, sharing a game, whose complicated rules
Are the only thing they can agree upon.

TROLL UNDER BRIDGE

It is almost dawn and the troll under the bridge
Gets to his knees, crawls out through the thin water
To the river bank. He is too old to catch billygoats,
Too old to threaten children at their play.
But he is not to old for one last thing:
To stay out and watch the sun rise
For the first time in his life—and the last.

FAIRIES IN A RING

One more turn, dear friends, one more,
And then we will be gone.
No one believes in us you see,
And all they want is lawn.

BLACK DOG TIMES

The world will end when the old woman
finishes her porcupine quill blanket,
though her black dog unpicks it whenever her
back is turned—Lakota legend

What can you do in these black dog times?
When the world is close to done,
And only the dog's teeth stand between us
And the ending? What can you do?
Choose to be born, stand up, pick the quills,
See through the mist, through the dark.
Sew yourself a robe, not a shroud.
Age gracefully. Take your medicine.
Have a colonoscopy. Do not complain.
Pick up your skirts, bend your aching knees,
And dance.

GREEN CHILDREN

Dazed they were, and scared,
lying on the cold stones,
their arms and legs green.
Not the dark green of ivy,
not the yellow green of apples
ripe on the summer bough,
nor the deep green of the ocean
where it leans against its bed.
They were the green of leeks,
of new-furled feather fern,
of the early leaf breaking soil.
When they opened their eyes,
their eyes were green, too,
and the little hairs on their arms
were inchworm green.
They spoke a green language
which the trees and flowers knew
but which we did not.

The boy died of a wasting,
the girl lived on,
eating broad beans,
forgetting her green tongue,
growing whiter with each day;

till she was christened
and married and all all white.
Not the white of milk
after the cream is skimmed off,
nor the white of October snow,
nor the white of a spring lily,
waxen and still,
nor the white of sea pearls
formed within the shell.
She was the white of the old moon
that shines over the hall.

THE RING AT YARROW

You take the pail,
I the jug,
and we will to Yarow
where the fairies dance
all in a ring
by the burnside.

We will offer them the drink,
whiter than milk,
redder than blood,
sucked from the nipple
closest to the heart.

We will dance all night,
our shoes worn through,
the little bones sticking
through the soles
like thorns on a rose.

Their stained glass wings
beating above us,
they will hold our necks
in their icy hands,
they will pump us

like small koo.

Our mouths pricked with kisses
sharper than serpent's bite,
sharper than gnats' teeth,
sharper than the venomed dart
of a southern tribe.

You take the pail
I the jug,
and we will to Yarow
this night and the next
and all the nights
till the moon burns down
behind our backs
and we leave our burnished bones as warning.

SWAN/PRINCESS

1.

When the change came
she was sitting in the garden
embroidering an altar cloth,
thin gold thread working the crown of Christ.
First her neck
arching like cathedral vaultings.
Dress ripping at the shoulders accommodated wings:
white-vaned, white-feathered like Oriental smocking.
Hands and feet tangling into orange legs,
inelegant, powerful as camshafts.
When her head went, she cried,
not for pain, but for the loss
of her soft, thin lips
so recently kissed by the prince.
Not even the sweet air,
not even earth unfolding beneath her
recompensed for those lost kisses
or the comfort of his human arms.

2.

When the change came
she was floating in the millpond,
foam like white lace tracing her wake.

First her neck shrinking,
candle to candleholder,
the color of old, used wax.
Wings collapsing like fans;
one feather left,
floating memory on the churning water.
Powerful legs devolving;
powerful beak dissolving.
She would have cried for the pain of it
had not remembrance of sky sustained her.
A startled look on the miller's face
as she rose naked and dripping,
recalled her to laughter,
the only thing she had really missed as a swan.

BEANS

Jack, you see, went hand over hand
To a land beyond understanding:
Streets paved with gold, gold bedsteads,
Gold bidets, golden harps, golden geese,
Eggs the color of wedding bands.
He hated being poor, having jack all.
So he stole a gigantic load, jacked the big man.
Has-been no longer, he unhanded himself
Down the beanstalk, fled home, kissed mom,
Drank a quick cup of something strong
Made from beans, then chopped down the stalk.
Sometimes a boy hits the jackpot,
Becomes a man with one lucky whack.
Believe it. Would a story lie?

3.
Telling the True

"Tell all the Truth, but tell it slant,
Success in circuit lies…"
—Emily Dickinson

THIS IS A STORY

This is a story,
but it is not my story:
There was first nothing,
and then more nothing,
and then an eternity of nothing.
Then out of that nothing
there came a light,
and a word,
and man.
And afterward,
part of the light
and part of the word
and part of the man
and part of the nothing
split off and became woman.

This is a story,
but it is not my story:
There was a god
who took his cock
and sprayed the nothing
and from those drops

came rams in the field,
and bulls, and boar,
and stallions, and stag,
and men.
And from those men
and rams,
and bulls, boar, stallions, and stag
and their many cocks spraying
there also came woman.

This is a story,
but it is not my story:
There was an egg
and out of that egg
there sprang men
with bows and spears
and stakes and clubs.
And wherever they shot
their many arrows,
and threw their spears,
and raked the earth
with their sharp stakes,
and beat it with their clubs
there appeared women.

This is a story,
but it is not my story,

which I carry in my secret place,
where there is no light
and no word
and especially no men.

WHEN RAVEN SANG

When Raven sang among the constellations,
fathers plucked their newborns,
red with birthblood,
from between the mothers' thighs,
saying, "He is already dying"
to fool the messengers of death.

My father did not see me
till the day after I was born;
did not hold me wrapped and diapered
till the day after that.

What is it about our men:
they cannot contain chaos,
they dare not trick the angels,
fearing to trade their own short lives
for the life of the newborn child.

WOMEN'S STORIES

There are two fathers I do not understand:
the one at the bridge,
devil's bargain still warm in his mouth,
kissing his daughter first, saying,
"Do I have a husband for you,"
and Abraham with his traitor's hand
leading Isaac to the hill to God.

These are not women's stories.
Even before I birthed my three,
and the one bled out before its time,
and the one encysted in the tube,
even before that I would have thrust the knife
in my own breast, before God;
I would have swallowed the kiss,
Gone back to the beast myself.

Job's wife had her own story.
Lot's pillar of salt cried tears
indistinguishable from her eyes.
Who invented a glass slipper
never had to dance.

Do not try to climb my hair.

Do not circle me with a hedge of thorns.
My stories are not your stories.
We women go into the desert together,
or not at all.

INTO THE WOOD

Let us enter the wood.
Take my hand.
I feel your fear
rise on your palm,
a map beneath my fingers.
Can you decipher
the pulsing code
that beats at my wrist?
I do not need to see
dragons
to know there are
dragons here.
The back of my neck knows,
the skin of my inner thighs.
There, among the alders,
between twin beeches,
the grey-white pilasters
twined with wild grape,
stands a pavilion,
inferior Palladian in style.
Who sleeps on the antique couch?
I hear a thin scraping,
a belly through dead leaves,
a long hollow good-by,

thin, full of scales,
modal, descending sounds.
In the dark
there will be eyes
thick as starshine, a galaxy of watchers
beneath the trailing vine.
And trillium,
the red of heart's blood,
spills between rocks
to mark the path.
Do not, for God's sake,
speak.
I know what is here
and what is not,
and if we do not
name it aloud
it will do us no harm.
So the spells go,
so the tales go,
and I must believe it so.

ONCE UPON

Once Upon A Time
there was a Wolf,
but not a Wolf,
an Other,
whose mother
and father were others,
who looked not like us,
Republican or Dem
in other words--
Them.
They were forest dwellers,
child sellers,
meat eaters,
wife beaters,
idol makers
oath breakers—
in other words, Wolf.
So Happy Ever After means
we kill the Wolf,
spill his blood,
knock him out,
bury him in mud,
make him dance
in red hot shoes.

For us to win
The Wolf must lose.

PRINCE CHARMING COMES

The goose flies past the setting sun, plums roasting in her
                   breast;
Sleeping Beauty lays her head a hundred years to rest.
Then fee, fi fo, the Giant fums
And to my dark Prince Charming comes
A ride, a ride, a ride, a riding,
Into my night of darkness, my own Prince Charming comes.

The witch is popped into the oven, rising into cake;
The Swan Queen glides her downy form to the enchanted lake.
And rum-pum-pum the drummer drums
As into darkness my love comes,
A ride, a ride, a riding,
Into my night of darkness, my own Prince Charming comes.

But do you come to take me out
Or come to put me in?
But do you come to yield to me
Or do you come to win?

It's half past twelve and once again the shoe of glass is gone,
And magic is as magic was and vanished with the dawn.
For Pooh has hummed his final hums,
The Giant finished off his fums.

They've drawn their final breath.
For into darkness my prince comes,
A ride, a ride, a ride, a riding,
Into the darkness my prince comes
On his bony horse called Death.

FAMILY STORIES

My father's stories
were tightly held.
He was stingy
with the past,
coining what
he could not remember,
parceling out the rest
with the cautious philanthropy
of a miser.
His lips moved
with the effort.

My mother's stories
waterfalled out
in little spurts
between apologies.
They were all praises,
Sunday school tales,
the morals
spoken in italics
so that we could not miss the points.
But we would not miss
the tellings.

Our old nurse Annie
had no tales
of her own,
only the ones
she had heard before.
She was not born
but made whole
to tell us stories.
Her past was one
filled with gods
and mothers-of-gods
and the little imp tales
that we loved the best.

My brother and I
are pieced together
like crazy quilts.
We keep warm
on winter evenings
with the weight
of all those tales.
But we never tell them
to one another.
We can't recall them,
only the ones that begin
"Do you remember when...
Do you remember?"

JANE YOLEN, often called "the Hans Christian Andersen of America," is the author of over 300 published books, including *Owl Moon, The Devil's Arthimetic,* and *How Do Dinosaurs Say Goodnight.* The books range from rhymed picture books and baby board books, through middle grade fiction, poetry collections, nonfiction, and up to novels and story collections for young adults and adults.

Her books and stories have won an assortment of awards—two Nebulas, a World Fantasy Award, a Caldecott, the Golden Kite Award, three Mythopoeic awards, two Christopher Medals, a nomination for the National Book Award, and the Jewish Book Award, among others. She is also the winner (for body of work) of the Kerlan Award, the World Fantasy Assn. Lifetime Achievement Award, and the Catholic Library's Regina Medal, and the 2012 du Grummond Medal. Six colleges and universities have given her honorary doctorates.

To learn more about her, visit her website at:
www.janeyolen.com

A MIDSUMMER NIGHT'S PRESS was founded by Lawrence Schimel in New Haven, CT in 1991. Using a letterpress, it published broadsides of poems by Nancy Willard, Joe Haldeman, and Jane Yolen, among others, in signed, limited editions of 126 copies, numbered 1-100 and lettered A-Z. One of the broadsides— "Will" by Jane Yolen—won a Rhysling Award. In 1993, the publisher moved to New York and the press went on hiatus until 2007, when it began publishing perfect-bound, commercially-printed books.

A MIDSUMMER NIGHT'S PRESS publishes poetry titles primarily under two imprints:

FABULA RASA: devoted to works inspired by mythology, folklore, and fairy tales. The first titles from this imprint are *Fairy Tales for Writers* by Lawrence Schimel, *Fortune's Lover: a Book of Tarot Poems* by Rachel Pollack, and now *Fairy Tales in Electri-city* by Francesca Lia Block.

BODY LANGUAGE: devoted to texts exploring questions of gender and sexual identity. The first titles from this imprint are *This is What Happened in Our Other Life,* by Lambda Literary Award-winner Achy Obejas; *Banalities* by Brane Mozetic, translated from the Slovene by Elizabeta Zargi with Timothy Liu; *Handmade Love* by Julie R. Enszer; and *Mute* by Raymond Luczak.